Junior Library of Money

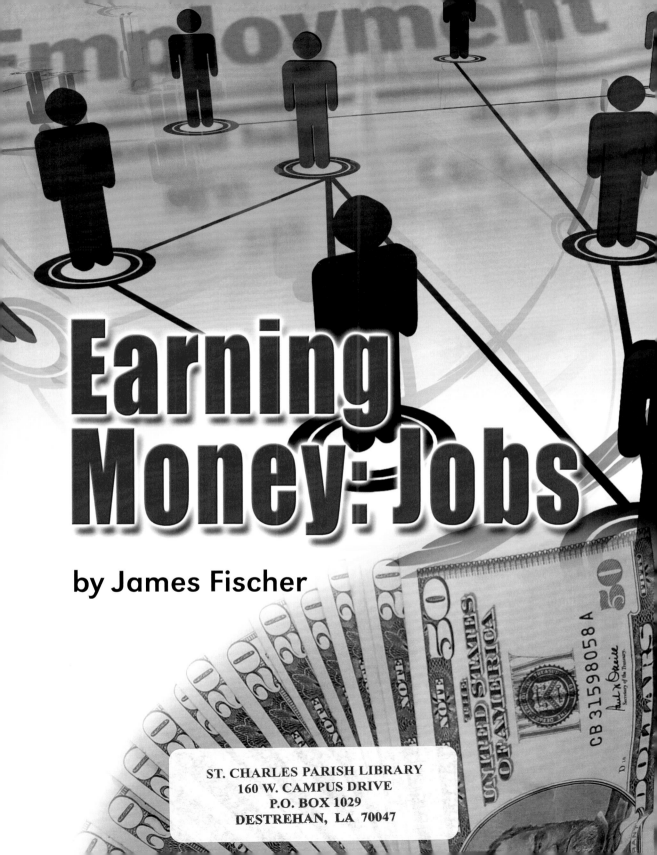

Earning Money: Jobs

by James Fischer

MASON CREST PUBLISHERS INC.
370 Reed Road
Broomall, Pennsylvania 19008
(866)MCP-BOOK (toll free)
www.masoncrest.com

First Printing
9 8 7 6 5 4 3 2 1

Library of Congress Cataloging-in-Publication Data

Fischer, James.
 Earning money : jobs / by James Fischer. – 1st ed.
    p. cm.
 Includes bibliographical references and index.
 ISBN 978-1-4222-1763-4 (hbk.)   ISBN 978-1-4222-1882-2 (pbk.)
 ISBN 978-1-4222-1759-7 (series)   ISBN 978-1-4222-1878-5 (pbk. series)
 1. Work–Juvenile literature. 2. Job hunting–Juvenile literature. 3. Employment interviewing–Juvenile literature. 4. Interpersonal relations–Juvenile literature. I. Title.
 HD4901.F455 2011
 650.1–dc22
                            2010028156

Design by Wendy Arakawa.
Produced by Harding House Publishing Service, Inc.
www.hardinghousepages.com
Cover design by Torque Advertising and Design.
Printed by Bang Printing.

Contents

Introduction

Our lives interact with the global financial system on an almost daily basis: we take money out of an ATM machine, we use a credit card to go shopping at the mall, we write a check to pay the rent, we apply for a loan to buy a new car, we set something aside in a savings account, we hear on the evening news whether the stock market went up or down. These interactions are not just frequent, they are consequential. Deciding whether to attend college, buying a house, or saving enough for retirement, are decisions with large financial implications for almost every household. Even small decisions like using a debit or a credit card become large when made repeatedly over time.

And yet, many people do not understand how to make good financial decisions. They do not understand how inflation works or why it matters. They do not understand the long-run costs of using consumer credit. They do not understand how to assess whether attending college makes sense, or whether or how much money they should borrow to do so. They do not understand the many different ways there are to save and invest their money and which investments make the most sense for them.

And because they do not understand, they make mistakes. They run up balances they cannot afford to repay on their credit card. They drop out of high school and end up unemployed or trying to make ends meet on a minimum wage job, or they borrow so much to pay for college that they are drowning in debt when they graduate. They don't save enough. They pay high interests rates and fees when lower cost options are available. They don't buy insurance to protect themselves from financial risks. They find themselves declaring bankruptcy, with their homes in foreclosure.

We can do better. We must do better. In an increasingly sophisticated financial world, everyone needs a basic knowledge of our financial system. The books in this series provide just such a foundation. The series has individual books devoted specifically to the financial decisions most relevant to children: work, school, and spending money. Other books in the series introduce students to the key institutions of our financial system: money, banks, the stock market, the Federal Reserve, the FDIC. Collectively they teach basic financial concepts: inflation, interest rates, compounding, risk vs. reward, credit ratings, stock ownership, capitalism. They explain how basic financial transactions work: how to write a check, how to balance a checking account, what it means to borrow money. And they provide a brief history of our financial system, tracing how we got where we are today.

There are benefits to all of us of having today's children more financially literate. First, if we can help the students of today start making wise financial choices when they are young, they can hopefully avoid the financial mishaps that have been so much in the news of late. Second, as the financial crisis of 2007–2010 has shown, poor individual financial choices can sometimes have implications for the health of the overall financial system, something that affects everyone. Finally, the financial system is an important part of our overall economy. The students of today are the business and political leaders of tomorrow. We need financially literate citizens to choose the leaders who will guide our economy through the inevitable changes that lie ahead.

Brigitte Madrian, Ph.D.
Aetna Professor of Public Policy and
Corporate Management
Harvard Kennedy School

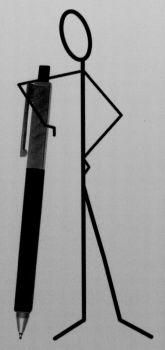

Why Work?

The reasons people work are often as varied as the kinds of jobs they have and the kinds of work they do every day. In many cases, you'll have to decide for yourself why you want to work, but the main reasons to work as a teenager are earning money, gaining work experience, and feeling independent.

Just about any job will let you earn a paycheck. You may want to work in order to save up for a car or so you can afford to go to the movies every weekend. Money can be a great motivation to work, even when you might not love what you're doing. At the most basic level, earning money is the reason that everyone works, whether to buy the things they want, provide for their families, or save for the future.

Money isn't all that you can get from your first job, however. By working, you gain experience that can help you find a better job later. Each time you learn how to do something new at your job, you're adding to the knowledge that you'll take with you in the future. Employers will want to hear about jobs you've had in the past and how they have shaped you and your skills when deciding whether or not to hire you. Starting to work as a teen can help you build up this kind of work experience early on in your life and assist you in getting work later on.

In addition to making money and gaining work experience, working at your first job can give you a sense of personal independence. It's not always easy to have a job as a teenager. Working takes a huge amount of commitment and responsibility, particularly when you consider school, homework, sports, afterschool activities, friends, and family. In many ways, working is a test of your strength of character. Are you able to make decisions effectively on your own? Can you make sure to get to work on time every day while keeping up with schoolwork? Working is a part of growing up and a great way to prove you can be independent and responsible.

How Old Do You Have to Be to Work?

In the same way that in order to drive you must be over the age of sixteen in most states, you must be over a certain age to work different kinds of jobs for differing lengths of time per week. Laws in the United States keep children from having to work, protecting them from being taken advantage of or being exposed to danger. Once you turn fourteen, you're able to work some jobs, but only people eighteen or older can work any job. Depending on your age, you'll be able to apply for different kinds of work.

If You're 14–15

Fourteen is the earliest age you're allowed to work in the United States. Teens who are between fourteen and fifteen years of age are able to work outside of school in jobs that aren't considered to be dangerous in any way. Before you turn sixteen, however, you'll have to work limited hours. This means no more than eight hours a day on the weekends and no more than three hours on school days, eighteen hours per week during school and forty per week in the summer.

Your state's labor department has much more information about the rules regarding what jobs young people are able to work and for how many hours.

DID YOU KNOW?

Visit youthrules.dol.gov/states.htm to find out more about these isses and many others affecting working teens.

If You're 16–17

At the age of sixteen you're able to do jobs that are considered non-hazardous, meaning that they aren't dangerous. The limits on the number of hours teens who are between fourteen and fifteen can work don't apply to those older than sixteen. Once you reach the age of sixteen, you'll be able to work for any number of hours, regardless of whether school is in session or not, with no limits placed on the number of hours you can work on school days or weekends. Many state governments require that workers under the age of eighteen have what are called employment certificates, also called working papers, documents that confirm your age and allow you to work.

If You're 18 or Older

Once you reach the age of eighteen, you're able to work any job you can find for any amount of time. You'll no longer have restrictions placed on the number of hours you're allowed to work and you can work jobs that may be considered hazardous (construction jobs, for example). At eighteen, you can work when and where you want.

DID YOU KNOW?

The U.S. Department of Labor has many resources online that young job seekers can use for free. Visit the DOL website at www.dol.gov/dol/audience/aud-kidsyouth.htm for more information about working, age restrictions, and labor laws.

What's the Right Job for You?

Finding your first job can be difficult in a few different ways. You might wonder about how you will be able to get your first job without having any work experience. You'll also have to decide whether to get a low-paying job to start with, or to aim higher and wait for something that pays better. First, however, you'll have to figure out what kind of work you want to do. This question has a lot to do with another: What do you want to get out of your first job?

Your first job might just be a way for you to make some money. That's perfectly fine, many people work simply to make enough money to live the way they want when they aren't at work. You might want to save up for that new mountain bike or enjoy eating out with friends every weekend, for example. A job can be much more than a way to make some cash to spend in your free time.

Beyond the paychecks you'll get at your first job, you'll also be gaining valuable work experience that can be used in your future career. If you're interested in business, for instance, there's no better way to learn the very basics of selling, exchanging money, and customer service than by working at a cash register.

In addition to money and experience, working your first job can be a great way to broaden your thinking when it comes to what you want to do in the long-term. For instance, you might think you'll hate flipping burgers and making fries. After a few weeks, you might be having the time of your life, leading you to want to become a chef. As well as changing your thinking about the kind of work you want to do, a job can help you to meet people you might not have met otherwise. You might find your coworkers become your new best friends. The boss you impress in your first job may go on to write you the glowing recommendation that gets you into the college you want to go to. You never know who you'll meet at a new job.

Deciding on what kind of work you want to do in your first job can be a tricky process. Thinking about what you want out of your first job,—whether it's new friends, money, or experience—is often the best way to narrow down your choices to those that appeal most to you.

When you're looking for work with a certain company, try checking with the Better Business Bureau to see if the company has

DID YOU KNOW?

had any complaints against it. Visit the BBB's website at www.bbb.org for more information about a wide range of businesses.

SELLING YOURSELF

You might think that you won't be able to get a job without having work experience, but often, what you enjoy doing when you're not working can be just as important. It's all about how you present the experience that you do have. Have you done any volunteer work? Played on a sports team? If you have, you've already learned a bit about the kind of teamwork, committment, and leadership that you'll need at a job. Adding **extracurricular activities** to a job application can often be a great way to get your foot in the door at your first job.

Here are a few other tips for finding work by using the skills you've built outside of work:

Volunteering: Letting potential employers know that you've got volunteer experience shows them that you're a dedicated person willing to help others without directly benefitting yourself. This kind of experience says a lot about you as a person.

Clubs and sports teams: Playing on a sports team can teach you teamwork and leadership.

Babysitting and tutoring: If you've looked after children or tutored other students, you've got experience being patient, helping others, and acting independently.

VOLUNTEERING

If you're not able to build the work experience you'd like to, perhaps because your age keeps you from working some jobs, volunteering can be a great way to get some experience to help you get your first job. You won't make any money volunteering, but you will gain skills and experience valuable in seeking paying jobs in the future.

FOR EXPERIENCE

When looking for volunteer work, try checking with local animal shelters, hospitals, clinics, church groups, or community organizations. Talking to your school's guidance and career counselors can also be a great way to find volunteer opportunities. School organizations like the student council can also provide volunteering experience in some cases. No matter where you end up volunteering, describing that experience in detail to employers is an excellent way to show them the kinds of skills you've developed.

So What's the First Step?

If you have questions about where you can find listings for open jobs in your local area, try talking to your school career counselor.

DID YOU KNOW?

She'll often be able to put you in touch with someone who can help or point you to resources you might not be aware of.

Once you've decided that you want to find a job, chosen what kind of work you think would be best for you, and gotten some experience either volunteering or through extracurricular activities, it's time to start searching for job openings. Where does somebody looking for work start? Here are a few examples of ways to find work:

Want Ads: Want ads featured in newspapers are advertisements for open jobs. Checking your local newspaper to find out about jobs in your area can be a great place to start your job search. Even if you don't find something that interests you, looking at want ads can give you a better idea of what work is available in your town or city, as well as the surrounding area.

Online: The internet has become a great resource for job seekers. There are a great many websites with information about the latest job openings in areas across the country. You'll be able to search for the jobs you might want to do and even post your resume on some sites, allowing potential employers to learn about you before you contact them.

Networking: Networking is often one of the best ways to find work. Reaching out to people you know and asking about their work experiences can help you narrow your own search. You might even find that they know about a job opening or can recommend you to someone they know who's looking to hire new workers. You never know until you ask!

DESCRIBING
YOUR
SKILLS

Job Application

Personal Information

NAME (LAST NAME FIRST)

SOCIAL

ADDRESS

CITY

PHONE NO.

EXPERIENCE

Lecklin KY, Transportation Entrepreneur, Kotka - *Full time job.* **August 19XX - September 19XX**
Responsible of 10-wheel truck as a driver in responsible position related to important functions of local Sawmill. Job consisted of taking care of truck, which was owned by employer. Value of that truck was approximately 100000± FIM. Main task was transporting sawdust to nearby located paper factory.

A.Ahlström OY, Cardboard Factory, Karhula - *Full time summer job.* **May 19XX - September 19XX**
Working in the factory and being part of manufacturing personnel department in various job tasks which included taking samples of cardboard, driving forklift and packaging finished products. Company had approximately 200 employees.

OY Wisapak AR, Papersack manufacturer, Karhula - *Full time summer job.* **June 19XX - July 19XX**
Working as assistant operator in manufacturing of papersacks. Continuos production of papersacks was required. Job was to take care of various tasks related to running the machine. I also did participate to packaging of finished products.

A.Ahlstrdm OY, Cardboard Factory, Karhula - *Summer job.* **July 19XX and June 19XX**
Working two consecutive summers in Cardboard factory. Tasks were mainly gardening and other duties involved to keep area clean and tidy. These jobs were performed before turning to required age of more demanding jobs in the factory.

HONORS
Maker and Creator of winning video presentation at competition organized by Kymenlaakson Chamber of Commerce 19XX. Being *representative* of Karhula High School. Task was to describe word competitiveness by video presentation.

MILITARY
Military Police, January 19XX - December 19XX. The eleven month period consisted 2 month basic training and 4 month training in N.C.O. training college. The remaining time as an military police small group leader in artillery army base. Responsibility was to take care of security in the army base and to lead, control and advice subordinates in their tasks.

LANGUAGES
! Finnish - *Native speaker*   ! English - *Fluent*   ! Swedish - *Proficient*

REFERENCES

Ioannis Toumas, Doctoral Student
J.L. Kellogg Graduate School
Chicago, Illinois
312-987-4567

Heikki Jarvinen, Personnel Director
A.Ahlström CY, Cardboard Factory, Karhula
Finland
358-52-789678

Bruno Cassiman, Doctoral Student
J.L. Kellogg Graduate School
Chicago, Illinois
312-987-4565

When creating your resume or filling out an application, you'll need to describe the experience and skills you have. There are a few key things to remember during this process. First, always be honest. You don't want to get the job by lying about the skills or experience you have. Being dishonest when looking for jobs will almost always backfire. Next, make sure to always keep your resume up to date. Keeping your information current is the only way to make sure potential employers get an accurate idea of who you are.

DID YOU KNOW

Though it may seem like something small, making sure that your resume and job application are free of spelling errors is very important.

Have a friend look over your application or resume to make sure everything is spelled correctly before you send it in.

Preparing for Your Interview

Remember!

The single most important thing to remember about job interviews is to prepare beforehand. Make sure you know about the company where you're applying (including what they do!). Having a few questions about the job or the company for the person who is interviewing you can be a great way to show that you are interested in the job and know at least a bit about the company's business. Asking specific questions about the company can also be a good way to show that you came to the interview prepared and informed. Be sure to know how to describe the skills and experience you have in a way that won't take up too much of the interview, as well.

It's a good idea to run through a few of the questions you might be asked in a job interview before you go. Try looking into a mirror so that you can practice confidently answering questions from potential employers. "Why do you want to work for us?" "What kind of extracurricular activities do you participate in?" "What is your greatest strength?" "Your greatest weakness?"

You might find that some questions you're asked in an interview can be difficult to answer, particularly if you're trying to give the interviewer the answers you think they want to hear. Instead of trying to say what you think the employer wants, try to be yourself. Be honest about your skills and experience, as well as why you want to work for the company and what your goals are. Make sure to get across why you'd be a good addition to the company's team, rather than how much you'd like to get paid. Asking how many vacation days you can expect is less likely to impress your interviewer than asking about the products that the company makes or sells. Let the interviewer know why you'd be a great pick.

If you are too personal in your answers to interview questions, you're less likely to come off as professional and business-minded.

DID YOU KNOW?

It's perfectly alright to be personable and warm, but telling an interviewer about your personal life can harm your chances of being hired.

Make a Good
First Impression

Making a good first impression is often one of the most important parts of seeking work. In our modern, interconnected world, first impressions aren't all about the way you look and act in person, either. Something as seemingly small as your email address can give someone an idea of what you're like that you may not want to present to the world. When looking for a new job, make sure that the email address you give to employers shows how professional and mature you can be. Think about using some variation of your name, rather than the name of your favorite band, song, animal, or activity. JamesSmith@email.com is a much more professional email address than SkaterDudeX@email.com. In addition to your email address, consider cleaning up information about yourself that you've posted online. Make sure that your Facebook photos and information shows the side of yourself that you want potential employers to see, for instance. You don't have to pretend to be someone you're not, but thinking about how people looking to hire you might see things can help you get an idea of the kind of information and image you want to put online. If you're going to become a part of a company or be hired at a business, you'll be acting as a representative of the people who work there and the organization itself. If your online profiles show you partying with your friends, employers might not want you as the face of their workplace.

DID YOU KNOW?

You'll often speak with potential employers over the phone before you meet with them face to face. It's important to keep this in mind when answering your phone. For instance, you definitely don't want to answer a call from someone who might want you to work for them by saying "What up!" Try to act professionally.

Interview Etiquette

Job interviews can be daunting, even scary, especially when you don't know about the unspoken rules of interview **etiquette**. Many of these rules may seem like common sense, but that doesn't make them any less important for you to remember when you're headed to an interview. Here are a few key examples of interview etiquette:

- *Dress to impress*: Before leaving for your interview, make sure that what you're wearing is appropriate and a bit more formal than what you might wear when hanging out with friends. You don't have to put on a bow tie or super high heels, but make sure that you don't show up in sweat pants and a t-shirt. Wearing too much cologne or perfume can also hurt more than it helps.

- *Arrive early*: It's always a good idea to arrive at an interview between ten and fifteen minutes early. This gives you a chance to prepare before your interview, but also gives the impression that you're interested in the job, **punctual**, and responsible.

- *Be polite*: It may seem obvious, but being polite can mean a lot in an interview. Make sure not to chew gum during the interview, for example. Keep your cell phone off during any job interview, as well.

- *Don't be a "no show"*: If you're unable to make it to an interview because something comes up, make sure you call ahead and let the interviewer know in advance. If you've been hired elsewhere, you should also inform your interviewer.

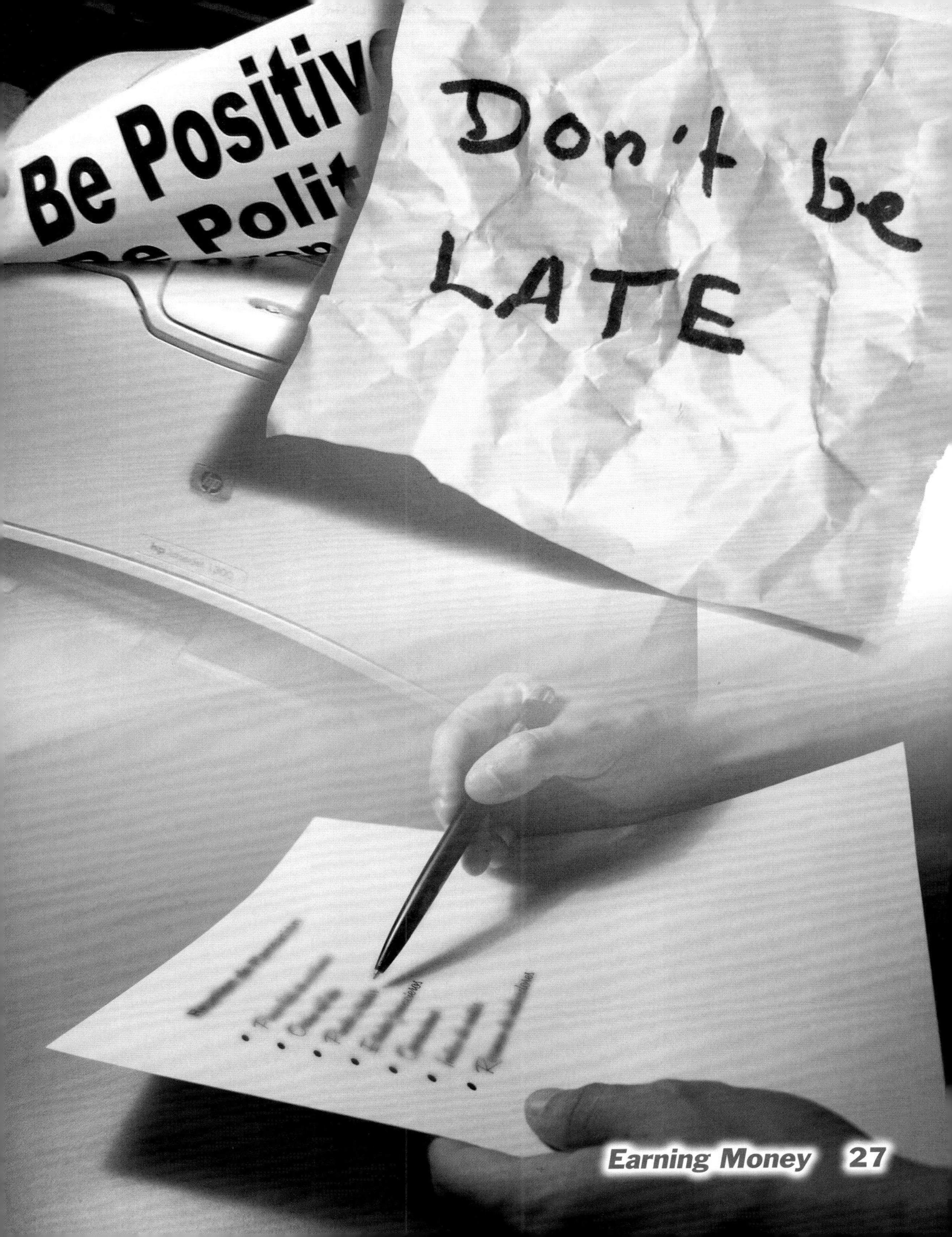
Be Positive
Polit
Don't be LATE

More Interview Tips

In addition to dressing well, showing up on time, and minding your manners, there are a few other things that you should keep in mind. Above all, you need to show confidence in your interview. If your interviewer thinks you look uncomfortable or sound overly nervous, they may not think you're the best person for the job. When you meet your interviewer, make sure to give him a firm handshake while maintaining eye contact, for example. While you're answering his questions, try to make your answers thoughtful, rather than jumping into a question before knowing what you're going to say.

One of the most important tips for succeeding in job interviews is a general one: Be aware of your body language and what it says about you. During your interview, it's entirely okay for you to be nervous, but make sure that your nerves don't get in the way of you getting the job. For instance, remember to always make eye contact with your interviewer. Fidgeting and biting your nails can give your interviewer and potential employer an impression you'd rather she not have of you. Instead, try to sit up straight, look at the interviewer, and keep still. This can help you to appear in control of the situation, even when you don't feel like you are. Talking to the interviewer in a respectful, calm, and friendly way is the best path to being hired. When the interview is over, remember to thank the interviewer for her time and consideration. If you don't hear back in a week or so, try calling to speak with her, and be respectful and professional during the call.

It's a good idea to write a letter to your interviewer thanking her again for her time, whether you think you got the job or not.

DID YOU KNOW?

This seemingly small kind of gesture can mean a lot to potential employers, and gives them a sense of the kind of person you are.

How Much Money Will I Earn?

When you're looking for your first job, it's important to keep your expectations for how much you'll make in check. This is not to say you shouldn't ever hope for more than minimum wage in a first job, but since often so many people are competing for jobs, understanding that you might not make as much as you'd like in your first job is important. Almost 70 million people, most of whom have more experience working hourly jobs than young people just starting to work, make their living by working hourly jobs in the United States. In many cases, the amount of work experience you have will determine how much you make, meaning that when you're just starting to search for work, you'll likely be earning the low end of what is possible. You may make more than minimum wage (the amount of money that has been established by the government as the lowest that a person can be paid per hour), and you may be able to **negotiate** with your new employers in order to make more money than they first offer you, but in general, it's a good idea to keep your pay request realistic. This is your first job after all. You've got a lot more time to work on making huge amounts of money in the future!

Though you're probably not going to get rich working your first job, here are a few reasons for you to be encouraged about your pay, today and tomorrow:

- According to the Bureau of Labor Statistics (BLS), nearly 98 percent of all workers who were paid hourly made more than minimum wage in 2006.

- Hourly workers often don't stay in jobs as long as workers who are paid salaries. This means that employers are looking for ways to hire new people and keep them on for longer periods of time. In many cases, workers who do a particularly good job are rewarded with pay raises, **bonuses**, or even promotions to higher positions. By being engaged and working hard, you're giving your employers reasons to pay you more.

- In addition to a paycheck, many employers give their employees benefits such as discounts on merchandise and free food. You may also be able to work out a flexible work schedule with your employer, something that can really help when juggling school, friends, and your other responsibilities.

- Work experience is **invaluable**. Working at a job that doesn't pay as much as you might like can seem like a drag, but it's often the best way to gain much-needed work experience. In addition, doing your job well and being courteous to your employers can earn you a glowing reference for when you're looking for your next job, or even applying to college.

Many states have set their minimum wages at higher levels than the national minumum wage, set by the federal government.

DID YOU KNOW?
To learn about your state's minimum wage, check out the Department of Labor's website at www.dol.gov/esa/minwage/america.htm.

Job Paperwork

When you first get your new job, you'll have to fill out a number of different forms. This paperwork, filled out before you actually start working but after you've been hired, is meant to get an accurate estimate of the amount of taxes you are supposed to pay each year. Money will be taken out of each of your paychecks to pay this amount. The form all

One of the many questions you'll need to answer when filling out all of the paperwork required of new employees is "How many dependants do you have?" This question is basically asking, "How many people depend on you to be their source of income?" If you're not married and don't have any children, you'll likely put down that you have no dependants. The number of dependants a person has affects the amount of taxes that he'll pay each year, but won't be of much concern to teens just starting to find work.

workers must fill out in order to have the correct amount of money taken out of each of their paychecks, is the W-4, and is provided by the U.S. Internal Revenue Service (the IRS), the government body responsible for collecting all taxes for the federal government. Filling out the W-4 form correctly is the best way to make sure you don't have to pay more taxes later.

Understanding Your Paycheck

You've gotten the job, worked your first couple weeks and received your first paycheck. But, what does it mean? If you've never seen a paycheck before, it can be a complicated, tangled mess of numbers, mysterious acronyms, and words you've never seen before. Don't worry, though, it's easy enough to understand your paycheck with a bit of information about all those numbers and acronyms. Here are explanations for a few of the more important pieces of information you might see on your paycheck:

Kerry Moss   **Perry Construction, LLC**   2455 N. Front Street Harborville, NY

Company PSTQ	Period Begin 3/13/2010	Division							
Number 6	Period End 3/26/2010	Branch							
Social Security #	Check Date 4/2/2010	Department							
Hire Date 10/28/2009	Check Number 607808	Team							

Earnings

Description	Location / Job	Rate	Hours	Current	Year To Date
Regular		9.50	20.00	190.00	1173.25
Total Earnings			20.00	190.00	1173.25
NET PAY		174.51	**Total Direct Deposits**		174.51

Deductions

Description	Current	Year To Date
Fed (S/0) (190.00)		1.91
OASDI (190.00)	11.78	72.74
Medicare (190.00)	2.76	17.01
NYS DBL	0.95	5.80
Dir Dep-Net Pay 00002XXXX	174.51	1075.79
Total Deductions	190.00	1173.25
Check Amount	0.00	0.00

- *Earnings*: Earnings refers to the amount of money you've made for the amount of time in that pay period (usually one or two weeks), before money is taken out for taxes.
- *Deductions*: Deductions refer to any money taken out of your account for federal and state taxes, Medicare (a program that helps pay for the medical care of older Americans), and **Social Security**.
- *Direct Deposit*: If you want, you can have some or all of your paycheck deposited straight into your bank account. This way you don't have to deal with depositing your check yourself.
- *Net Pay*: Your net pay is the amount of money that you actually take home after deductions.

If you're still unsure about the way certain information is presented on your paycheck, you can visit www.snagajob.com/uploadedfiles/SnagAJob.com-First-job-guide.pdf and read the "Breaking Down the Paycheck" section to find out more.

Where Did the Money Go?

Money Go?

TAX

Each time you get paid at your new job, some of the money you make will be taken out of your paycheck to go to the federal and state goverments to pay for things like roads, schools, and the military. Every person who works needs to pay taxes from their paychecks. The amount of money taken out of your pay is based on your answers to the questions asked on the paperwork you filled out when you were first hired. This amount is an estimate of the amount of taxes you'll owe each year.

In addition to the taxes you pay that go to building things like bridges or schools, some money goes to Social Security (a program that gives assistance to older Americans). Some money may also be taken out to pay for any benefits you receive, such as medical or dental care.

The money that is taken out of each paycheck is based on an estimate of the taxes you'll owe each year. Because it's only an estimate, however, it may not be exact. In order to sort out how much you actually owe, you need to file a tax return with the Internal Revenue Service, the IRS, the group which collects taxes for the government. Your tax return will determine whether you owe more in taxes, or if you get a refund check because you paid more than you owed.

If you have any questions about paying taxes or having money taken out of your paycheck, the Internal Revenue Service's website

DID YOU KNOW?

has a lot of information you may find helpful. Visit www.irs.gov to find out more about how taxes work and how you should file your return.

On-the-Job Questions

After being hired, you'll find that you need to ask questions in order to find out all the things you need to know about the company, your job, and many details you'll need to know. You should never feel like you can't ask questions of your boss or coworkers. They aren't going to think less of you because you need to ask a few questions. In most cases in fact, your employer and co-workers would prefer you ask questions early, rather than have you make a mistake because you didn't ask. Each company has its own rules and methods of doing things, all of which you'll need to know.

Here are some of the kinds of questions you should ask your boss or coworkers when you start a new job:

- When do I get paid and how often?
- How will I get paid? Is there a direct deposit option? Direct deposit means that your paycheck will be put into your bank account automatically.
- How do I keep track of the number of hours I'm working?
- What should I do if a customer complains about the company and/or wants to speak to a manager?
- What should I do if I have an accident or get hurt while on the job?
- What should I do if I need to stay home sick or if I miss a shift for any reason?
- For full-time hourly or summer jobs, you'll want to ask how much time off you get and how much notice you'll need to give. You also want to find out how much notice you need to give before you leave for the summer or school year. And if you want to be able to come back to the job for summer or seasonal work, set the ground work early and let them know you're interested.

Make sure to ask questions at a time that is convenient for others, rather than firing off a list of questions while your coworkers are busy doing something else. In general, however, your employer should be happy to clear up any confusion you might have about any aspect of your job, so don't be afraid to ask if you need some explanation.

How Should You Dress for Work?

You already know that acting in a professional way while looking for work and while on the job is extraordinarily important, but what exactly does it mean to act professionally? Professional behavior comes in many different forms. What you wear, for instance, is a reflection of your attitude, committment, and level of professionalism.

In the majority of cases, what you should be wearing to work will be covered by the company's dress code. Most workplaces have a unique dress code that will spell out exactly what is allowed and what cannot be worn at work. At some jobs, you might be given a uniform to wear while you're at work. If you have a uniform you must wear at work, it's up to you to keep that uniform clean and undamaged. In other jobs, employers might want you to wear your own clothes, but have specific rules about what can and cannot be worn. Work dress codes will also often cover what types of jewelry are allowed and how workers can wear their hair while at work. No matter what the rules of your workplace when it comes to clothing, your employer will make them absolutely clear to you before you come in for your first day of work.

In addition to making sure that the clothes you wear are appropriate for your work environment, it's important that you keep them clean. No one wants to work with someone who is wearing a uniform that has gone unwashed for a week. The way you present yourself, in a sense, shows the level of respect you have for your employers, coworkers, and customers. Showing up in wrinkled, dirty clothes smelling like you haven't showered in days might give others the idea that you don't really care about the job or the people you work with. Often, what you wear and how you wear it are equally important when considering how others will see you while you're at work. Looking your best is a great way to show your commitment to the job.

How to Impress Your Boss

Impressing your boss can be a great way to get ahead in almost any job you'll have. In most cases, this means working hard and doing your job well. Your boss will judge you on how well you do your job more than almost anything else, but there are other ways of showing her just how dedicated you are to your work. Here are a few tips that can help you make a great impression on your boss, and stay on her good side as long as you work for her:

1. Arrive early. Arriving for work before you're expected is a great way to have time to prepare for your shift, but it also shows that you're interested in your job and eager to get to work, both of which your boss will appreciate.

2. Always be honest. If you make a mistake, don't try and cover it up or lie to get out of trouble. Taking responsibility for your own actions will reflect

well on you. Earning the trust of your boss and coworkers is vital in any job. Once you lose the faith of your employers and fellow employees, it can be very hard—if not impossible—to gain it back.

3. Help others out. Your boss will notice if you're being helpful to your co-workers or to your employers. He'll also remember that time you took on extra work without complaint when you were asked.

4. Show, don't tell. Instead of telling your boss and coworkers about how well you're doing your job, try to make it clear to them how effectively you're able to fulfill your responsibilities.

5. Make sure your boss knows you care. Caring about your coworkers helps everyone work better together. Always act respectfully towards others and your boss will notice your kindness. Keep in mind, teamwork is the core of many work environments.

6. Think outside the box. Although you may be younger than some of your coworkers, you should always feel free to offer your own thoughts when it's appropriate. Speaking your mind shows your boss that you're thinking critically about your work.

7. Do your job well. No matter what job you've got, take pride in your work. Think of your work as a reflection of you. If you're washing dishes, making sure those dishes get as clean as possible is the best way to get yourself noticed. Remember, the effort you put into your work is often how you'll be judged by your employers.

How to NOT Impress Your Boss

Just as there are many small things you can do to impress your boss by proving how valuable a worker you are, there are a number of things you might do that can offend your employer, making it less likely you'll get paid more, promoted, or recommended for other work. Knowing what to avoid when in a work setting can often be just as helpful as knowing what you should be doing. Here are some things that your boss will definitely frown upon:

1. Asking about money. It's completely fine to ask about how much you're going to be paid at a job, but make sure that you aren't asking at an inappropriate time (it's

not the best opening question to ask an interviewer, for instance). In addition, constantly asking when you're getting paid, why you aren't making more, or if you can have a raise, is likely to get you noticed—but not in the way you might want. Everyone works for money, but focusing only on the paycheck you get every two weeks is the fastest way to get on your boss's nerves.

2. Taking the day off without informing others. If you get sick or need to take the day off for any other reason, make sure you tell coworkers or your boss. Not showing up at work, and then not calling to tell anyone at your work why, can make your boss less likely to give you hours and also give him a reason to think you aren't responsible or dedicated to the job.

3. Arriving late. Coming to work late shows that you don't care enough to arrive on time. Getting to work late once in a while is usually fine, but repeatedly arriving late tells your boss you're less than responsible.

4. Not caring for yourself. Making sure you present yourself in the best way possible is an important part of getting a job, but it's also important in impressing your boss. Coming to work in a dirty uniform, for instance, is a quick way to leave your boss and coworkers with a negative impression. Make sure you are taking care of your personal hygiene and wearing clean clothes when you come to work.

What If You're Sick?

Everyone gets sick occasionally, and everyone will likely need to take a day off from work to stay home sick at some point. Though there's no problem with taking a sick day every once in a while, taking too many, or simply lying about being sick, can lead to your employer thinking less of your abilities, or even cost you your job.

Taking a day off can be a good way to get some rest before returning to work. If you're contagious, meaning that others could get sick from being around you, you should definitely stay home. Some medicines may negatively affect your ability to do your job as well, so employers will understand if you stay home while on these types of medication. In addition, your doctor may suggest you stay home to get better. In this case, taking the doctor's advice is the best way to go. If you take the day off, however, you're probably not going to get paid for it. Taking too many days off can also make your boss unhappy. When just starting a new job, it's really best to go to work as much as you can, to make a good impression on your new employer. So try not to take a day off unless you absolutely need to.

What Is Harassment?

Harassment is an unfortunate reality in many workplaces. The word "harassment" refers to any behavior that upsets or offends another person in any way. The best thing for you to do as a new worker is to find out how the company you work for defines harassment, and what you should do if you are a victim or know someone who is. In general, you should always be aware of the way you're acting at work and be respectful to your coworkers. Remember to always treat people in the way you would want to be treated. In most cases, harassment policies are explained to new employees when they start work.

Though harassment covers a wide range of offensive behavior, sexual harassment is particularly serious. Sexual harassment refers to any sexual

DID YOU KNOW?

speech or behavior that is unwanted and offensive, including any harassment based on gender or sexual orientation.

Juggling Your Responsibilities

The life of the average teenager is much busier than many people might think. After taking into account the time it takes to go to school, play on sports teams, attend extracurricular activities, and complete homework, it's a wonder teens have any time left for friends and fun. Adding a part-time job to the mix can seem overwhelming, but there are many employers who understand that teens have other responsibilities besides working. Part-time jobs in restaurants, for instance, often allow workers to have flexible schedules. Many restaurants need workers for nights and weekends—often their busiest times—so teenagers who need to go to school during the day have many chances to work. In addition, jobs at retail stores can be a good fit for students who need time for things like school and homework. Letting your employer know about your schedule is very important, for them and for you. Working together, you'll likely be able to come up with a **routine** that allows you to juggle all of your responsibilities successfully.

When figuring out your weekly schedule, make sure that you're factoring in enough time for sleep. If you work on school nights, try having your homework done before you go to work so that you don't have to do it when you get home. Getting enough sleep is important for teens in school, since the amount of sleep you're getting each night makes a difference in how well you'll do in class. Most experts recommend that you get around seven or eight hours of sleep every night.

If you're worried about getting all of your school work done, hanging out with friends, and working a few shifts a week, try working fewer hours to start out. When you know more about how much time you'll have each week, you can ask for more hours.

Managing Your Time

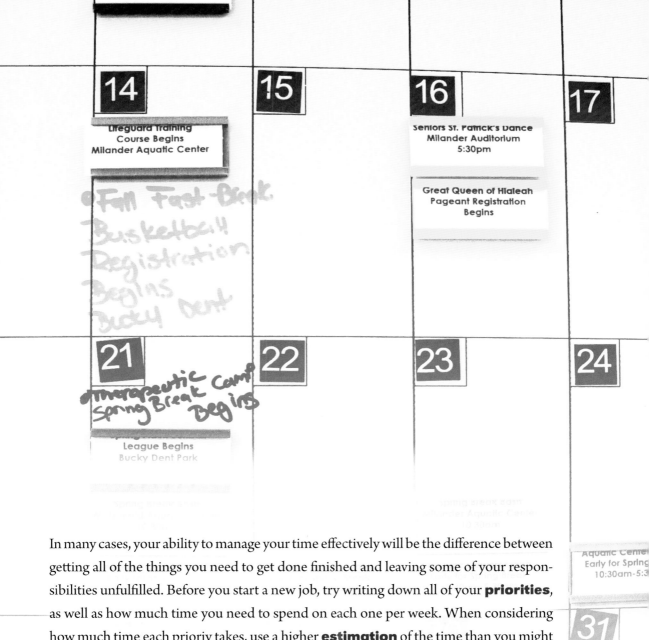

14	15	16	17
Lifeguard Training Course Begins Milander Aquatic Center		Seniors St. Patrick's Dance Milander Auditorium 5:30pm	
•Fall Fast-Break Basketball Registration Begins Bucky Dent		Great Queen of Hialeah Pageant Registration Begins	

21	22	23	24
•Therapeutic Camp Spring Break Begins League Begins Bucky Dent Park			

In many cases, your ability to manage your time effectively will be the difference between getting all of the things you need to get done finished and leaving some of your responsibilities unfulfilled. Before you start a new job, try writing down all of your **priorities**, as well as how much time you need to spend on each one per week. When considering how much time each prioriy takes, use a higher **estimation** of the time than you might think each takes, just to rule out any chance you'll not have enough time to complete what you need to. Then set aside some time each week for activities you enjoy, such as hanging out with friends, going to the movies, or surfing the Internet. Once you know how much time you've got left, you can decide how much of that time you want to spend working. Make sure to stick to your schedule once you've made it!

Where Do You Go From Here?

Getting your first paycheck can bring with it an amazing feeling of financial independence, a feeling that the time you spent working has paid off, that you can make your own way through dedication to hard work. Working can benefit you in many other ways besides a paycheck as well, perhaps motivating you to decide on a career, rethink your priorities, or set you on a path you didn't expect to follow. Once you understand the benefits of working as a teenager, and how working as a young person can help you in the future, you can set about making your job what you want it to be. Want to make more money? Try to show your boss and coworkers that you're committed and worthy of a raise. Want to take work experience and a recommendation to your next job? Ask questions about things you're not sure of, taking in as much information as you can. As is the case in sports, school, or friendships, what you put into a job will determine what you take from it.

WORK

As you continue to work, whether remaining in your first job or trying out many different jobs over time, it's important that you build and maintain strong relationships with the people you work with and for. Your first boss may help you get your second job or write you a college recommendation. Your co-workers may become your contacts when you're searching for work through **networking** in the future.

The jobs you have as a teenager, and your first job specifically, will leave a lasting impression on you for the rest of your life. In many ways, your first job will influence how you see working in general. Work is an important part of growing into responsible adulthood, and your first job is a big step on that journey.

Here's What You Need to Remember

• Getting a job can be a great way to earn some money, gain valuable work experience, and get a sense of what you want to do in your future career.

• Though you might worry that you don't have enough work experience to get a job in the first place, consider all of the extracurricular activities in which you participate. Play on a sports team? You're learning about teamwork. Volunteer on the weekends? You're learning dedication and self-motivation. These skills will serve you well when applying for your first job.

• Once you've figured out what kind of work you want to do, try looking in the newspaper or online for job openings. You can also ask the people you know or your school career counselor for help.

• In your first interview, make sure you're giving the right impression. Wear nicer clothes than you might when hanging out with friends. Being polite and professional can help show you in the best light possible.

•Once you've landed the job, make sure that you are aware of the company rules. Feel free to ask questions if need be. Doing your job well and being respectful of others is the best way to impress your employers (as well as your coworkers) and get the most out of your new job.

Words You Need to Know

bonuses: Extra money that an employee receives as a reward for good work.

estimation: The amount of time, for example, that you think a job will take to complete based on how complicated it is and how fast you work.

etiquette: Polite and appropriate behavior for a particular situation.

extracurricular activities: Clubs, sports, performance groups, etc., in which a student participates in addition to their regular schoolwork.

invaluable: Something worth a lot, and not easily replaced.

negotiate: To discuss something in order to reach an agreement.

networking: Using the help of people you know to locate job opportunities and introduce or recommend you to potential employers.

priorities: Those things that are considered most important.

punctual: On-time and reliable.

routine: A schedule of your daily activities that is efficient and predictable.

Social Security: A number of government programs for sick, disabled, and retired workers that is paid for by taking money out of the pay of people currently employed.

Further Reading

Byers, Ann. *Great Resume, Application, and Interview Skills*. New York: Rosen Publishing, 2008.

Coon, Nora E. *Teen Dream Jobs: How to Find the Job You Really Want Now!* Hillsboro, Oreg.: Beyond Words Publishing, 2003.

Frisch, Carlienne. *Everything You Need to Know About Getting a Job*. New York: Rosen Publishing, 1999.

Harmon, Daniel E. *First Job Smarts*. New York: Rosen Publishing, 2009.

Pervola, Cindy & Debby Hobgood. *How to Get a Job If You're a Teenager*. Janesville, Wis.: Upstart Books, 2000.

Slomka, Beverly. *Teens and the Job Game: Prepare Today—Win It Tomorrow*. Bloomington, Ind.: iUniverse, 2007.

Wilkes, Donald L. *Teen Guide Job Search: Ten Easy Steps to Your Future*. Bloomington, Ind.: iUniverse, 2006.

Find Out More On the Internet

"How to Land Your First Job"
www.snagajob.com/teen-jobs/first-job.aspx

"Job Interview Tips for Teens"
www.moneyinstructor.com/art/interviewteens.asp

"Most Common Job Interview Questions for Teens"
www.millionaire-kids.com/interviewquestions.html

"Teen Interview Tips"
jobsearch.about.com/od/interviewsnetworking/a/teeninterview.htm

"Teen Job Search Tips—Job Search Tips for Teenagers"
jobsearch.about.com/od/teenstudentgrad/a/teenjobsearch.htm

"Tips for Teens: How to Find Your First Real Job"
www.quintcareers.com/teen_first_job.html

The websites listed on this page were active at the time of publication. The publisher is not responsible for websites that have changed their address or discontinued operation since the date of publication. The publisher will review and update the websites upon each reprint.

Index

Photo Credits

About the Author and Consultant

James Fischer received his master's in education from the State University of New York, and went on to teach life skills to middle school students with learning disabilities. Money management and financial skills were a major part of his emphasis in the classroom. He has applied these skills to his writing for this series.

Brigitte Madrian is Professor of Public Policy and Corporate Management in the Aetna Chair at Harvard University's Kennedy School of Government. She has also been on the faculty at the Wharton School and the University of Chicago. She is also a Research Associate at the National Bureau of Economic Research and coeditor of the *Journal of Human Resources*. She is the first-place recipient of the National Academy of Social Insurance Dissertation Prize and the TIAA-CREF Paul A. Samuelson Award for Scholarly Research on Lifelong Financial Security.